T0114998

A Simple Book

Zycos

iUniverse, Inc.
New York   Bloomington

A Simple Book

iUniverse books may be ordered through booksellers or by contacting:

*iUniverse
1663 Liberty Drive
Bloomington, IN 47403
www.iuniverse.com
1-800-Authors (1-800-288-4677)*

*Because of the dynamic nature of the Internet, any Web addresses or links
contained in this book may have changed since publication and may no longer
be valid.*

*ISBN: 978-1-4502-6916-2 (sc)
ISBN: 978-1-4502-6917-9 (ebk)*

Printed in the United States of America

iUniverse rev. date: 10/29/2010

WISH
SUCCESS TO
SOMEONE
ELSE

GIVE A NICE COMPLIMENT TO A TOTAL STRANGER

PLANT
A
TREE

PLANT
SOME
FLOWERS

GIVE
LOTS OF
HUGS

FORGIVE SOMEONE FOR HARMS THEY MAY HAVE CAUSED YOU

FORGIVE
YOURSELF
FOR HARMS
YOU MAY
HAVE
CAUSED
OTHERS

PRAY

LISTEN TO
OTHERS
INSTEAD OF
WAITING
TO SPEAK

EAT
FRUITS
AND
VEGETABLES

DRINK
TEA

TELL
A
CLEAN
JOKE

THINK
AND ACT
WITH
SAFETY IN
MIND

VISUALIZE POSITIVE OUTCOMES TO EVENTS

BELIEVE
IN
YOURSELF

BELIEVE
IN THE
GOODNESS
WITHIN
OTHERS

TURN LEMONS INTO LEMONADE

EXERCISE
REGULARLY

DANCE

SING

UNDERSTAND
THAT THE
UNIVERSAL
POWERS ARE
HERE TO
HELP YOU

ORGANIZE YOUR OFFICE

CLEAN
YOUR
HOUSE

TAKE
A
NAP

BREATHE THE ENERGY AROUND YOU

GO
FOR
A
WALK

ENCOURAGE
OTHERS
TO DO WELL

HOPE AND
OPTIMISM
ARE
POWERFUL
FORCES -
ALWAYS KEEP
THEM CLOSE

PARTICIPATE
IN HELPING
TO KEEP
YOUR
COMMUNITY
CLEAN

LEARN TO
PLAY A
MUSICAL
INSTRUMENT

OPEN YOUR
MIND TO
ADVICE,
SUGGESTIONS
AND
IDEAS
FROM
OTHERS

OBSERVE
WITHOUT
PRECONCEPTIONS
OR
EXPECTATIONS

DEVELOP A GOOD SENSE OF HUMOR- LAUGHTER HEALS

SHARING
OPENS
DOORS TO
WONDERFUL
GIFTS OF
FRIENDSHIP

FULLY
COMPREHEND
THE VALUE
OF
TEAMWORK

BE GRATEFUL
FOR ALL
OF YOUR
BLESSINGS

IN DEALING
WITH OTHERS
MAKE SURE
EVERYONE
BENEFITS

AVOID
MAKING
ASSUMPTIONS

ACTS OF KINDNESS CREATE AMAZING ENERGY

IN TIMES OF
UNCERTAINTY
AVOID
RUSHING
OR FORCING
EVENTS -
WAIT UNTIL
THINGS
BECOME
CLEAR

TALK TO A FRIEND WITH WHOM YOU HAVE NOT SPOKEN IN A WHILE

AVOID
BURNING
BRIDGES

SAY THANK YOU

LIVE
AND
LET
LIVE

UNDERSTAND
THE
BEAUTY
OF
SIMPLICITY

LEARN HOW TO PREPARE FRESH AND HEALTHY FOOD

RESPECT
ALL
LIVING
CREATURES

LEARN
ANOTHER
LANGUAGE

BE QUICK TO APOLOGIZE AND MAKE AMENDS FOR MISTAKES

VIEW CRITICISM AS AN OPPORTUNITY TO LEARN, CHANGE AND GROW

DO NOT
TAKE
THINGS
TOO
PERSONALLY

BE CAREFUL
WITH YOUR
CHOICE OF
WORDS -
THEY CARRY
GREAT
POWER

ACCEPT WHAT YOU CANNOT CHANGE

UNDERSTAND
THE
POWER
OF
PATIENCE

TRUE
STRENGTH
LIES IN
NON-VIOLENCE

DO YOUR
BEST
NOT TO
WASTE

BE CAREFUL
ABOUT
JUDGING
THE PAST.
KNOWLEDGE
LEARNED
THROUGH
MISTAKES IS
QUITE COMMON
AND
OFTEN RESULTS
IN A BETTER
BEING

BE CAREFUL IN
JUDGING
APPEARANCES-
LOOK
INSIDE
FOR THE
TRUTH

VIEW
SITUATIONS
NOT JUST
FROM YOUR
PERSPECTIVE
BUT FROM
THE
PERSPECTIVE
OF OTHERS
INVOLVED

STAY
FLEXIBLE,
BOTH IN MIND
AND BODY.
BETTER TO
BEND THAN
TO BREAK

HAPPINESS
IS OUR
PERSONAL
RESPONSIBILITY

ALWAYS
GIVE A
LITTLE
EXTRA

DREAM

WRITE
A
POEM

USE MISTAKES AND BAD DECISIONS AS OPPORTUNITIES TO IMPROVE YOUR JUDGMENT

GROOVE IS
HEART, MIND
AND BODY
WORKING
TOGETHER
AS ONE -
GET YOUR
GROOVE ON

LIFE IS
A MYSTERY-
ENJOY
THE
MYSTERY

DEVELOP
FAITH AND
TRUST IN
YOUR MIND
AND BODY AS
A HEALING FORCE
FOR
OTHERS AS
WELL AS
YOURSELF

SPEND QUALITY TIME IN NATURE

LISTEN TO
YOUR
INSTINCTS,
FEELINGS AND
INTUITION -
MANY TIMES
THEY CAN STEER
YOU IN
THE RIGHT
DIRECTION
BETTER THAN
WHAT SEEMS
"SENSIBLE"

STAY SMALL - AVOID ARROGANCE AND SUPERIORITY OF THOUGHT

BE AWARE OF
AND
UTILIZE
YOUR
RESOURCES

ENCOURAGE
AND
WELCOME
LONG
TERM
RELATIONSHIPS

LIVE
WITHIN
YOUR
MEANS

WHAT CAUSES THE VARIOUS EXPRESSIONS OF MIND? WHERE DO THEY COME FROM?

TO
LISTEN
IS TO
LEARN

ENJOY
QUIET

LOVE UNCONDITIONALLY